Poems of Essence:
Life, Love & Pain

by
Marie Skilling

Published by

Picouture Press

To My Brother,

Your unbridled support has got me through.

You are my inspiration!

Being true to oneself takes the least effort of all.

Table of Contents

Acknowledgments

I thank my brother, as he was the first person to read this book of poems. He was the only person I could release the control to in the beginning, without needing to read them aloud to him. The reason; he loves me no matter what, he wants everything there is in life for me, and I feel safe. I offer the same to him, in support of his dreams.

I must therefore also thank our wonderful parents, for nurturing such an unbreakable bond, and for loving us so very deeply.

Thank you to Mette, my dear Danish friend that I met in India. She was the first person that I could ever read my work aloud to, as an adult. Granted, she had to lie on the bed whilst I sat on the floor with my back to her, but it was a first step.

Many people were loving listeners of my excitement in this process; I thank you. Readers of www.picouture.com read some of these poems before they went to print. Particularly in the case of 'Earth Meets Mars', I have to thank the Thirty Seconds to Mars' Echelon tribe, for their support in promoting this poem. But all readers, all those that subscribe to my blog, and all my friends and family that read, comment and enjoy my poems, thank you.

Thanks to Kat for introducing me to the mighty Echelon, for making sure I don't get too serious, and for making me laugh so hard I nearly pee. I have written down our antics young lady; you will find them printed one day.

Thanks go to Anisha, for our coffee and tea mornings that merge into afternoon tea, followed by a move to the local brassiere where we watch people passing by, and muse over our thoughts, or my next romantic idea. The rainy days have been made easier in her company.

To Rhia, my beautiful friend I cannot imagine life without: No matter where I am, no matter how far, you are always so close to me. You are everlasting, and I cherish you so very much. Thank you for your support, love, kindness and laughs. And thank you for bringing me closer to your loving mother, it's a real treat to spend time with 'Gemini Genes'.

I thank my editor, Sally Munson for giving me her critical eye and loving heart. I was also lucky enough to have some eager reviewers. They all provided me with valuable insight; they know who they are, and I am very grateful to them.

Thank you to those people that have made my life difficult, giving me a reason to search my soul, to find better for myself.

Thank you to those that that have seen my pain, and lifted it, in all shapes and forms.

Thank you to India for touching me so very deeply. And thank you to Shri Kali Ashram for providing the very best medicine life has to offer: an opportunity to love oneself.

Thank you to all the people and experiences that have influenced my poems.

And thank you for taking the time to read my poems; I hope you really feel a sense of how my heart spills.

Introduction

Poems of Essence:
An expression of my journey; the darkness, the light, the love, and the dreams.

In these poems you will discover my creative essence, my whole self displayed in poetic form.

Since I was a child, I have been told that my smile lights people's faces. However, it took me a while to accept, nurture, and then love the person behind the smile - to find the light that others see.

Poems of Essence:
A collection of words, written in the beginning, during a time of deep self-discovery. I have continued to write, enjoying every moment, allowing my mind and heart to peacefully wander through ideas, word, and rhyme.

I love writing, I always have, and now I allow myself this pleasure by not controlling how it works out. I now find the courage to share wholly with you.

For me and for you, I give you:
Poems of Essence.

The Poems

Each poem has been inspired by the life I have lived.

Life

Living Light

In India alone
A story unfolds
A self to discover
A heart to recover.

No tragedy escapes
As pain resurrects
But in finding it here
The light invades.

As heaven inspires
And dreams stir revolt
Life long desires
Appear with a bolt.

It happens in awe
Of magnificent scenes
As nature prevails
And worries are paled.

For all that matters
Is where it should be
Complete in myself
To always be free.

Earth Meets Mars

Thank you to Thirty Seconds to Mars for an
amazing concert in Lille, France.

The stars aren't as far
As the Moon or Mars
They're here in the dark
Shining golden shards.

From the Night of the Hunter
To the depths of a crowd
A trio emerge -
Confident, proud.

A whirling Messiah
Brings a Hurricane's rage
As sweat powered muscles
Drum the crowd to the stage.

A kingdom unites
In loving trance
As Kings meet Queens
In song and dance.

Under the strength of 100 suns
The faint of heart fall foul of heat
As mighty Mars beat tribal bars
And ravaged fans push hard and deep.

For an Echelon throne
A God to surrender
To the Moon and stars
One night to remember.

Saluted Spark

A fiery sun burns deep within
To heat the heart -
Salute, begin.

A Moonlit night fills opened eye
To see the bliss
Of true divine.

A sacred spark ignites the soul
To feel the light
And sense it grow.

A Loving breeze blows soft on skin
To tell the soul
To breathe it in.

Flowing waves soothe tired minds
For sacred selves
To shine their light.

Heat the heart
That feeds the soul
To see the light
Of all divine.

Harmonious Sin

A rib of sin
Delivers fear
Of separation
From creation.

Deny thy self
Our true desires
Forsake our hearts
For thy Messiah.

But this is not
The story told:
Just politics
From times of old.

Control our race
Repress our souls
Tell us lies
In name of grace.

But he who speaks
In absolute
Knows we join
As one complete.

Divine we are
To serve our soul
In harmony
We reach our goals.

A Crow Told Me

A crow stopped by
To peck a seed
Fallen from the sky.

He paused his step
To look at me
And tell me to be free.

His buddy came
To join the fun
And nod to seal the point.

That life is love
And love is true
When you stop to see –

The beauty and the rhythmical:
Your body knows it all
Your mind just has to catch your heart
To really make a call.

The crows can see -
They smile at me
And then they fly away.

They leave me with my happy self
To light my every way.

Indian Days

Upon soft sand our bodies lie
Finding form in rhythmic flow
And grateful bliss of all there is
As gentle breeze does softly blow.

A bow of sorts, releases life
A wheel then rolls it to the sky
Where Eagles fly above our heads
And butterflies, they flutter by.

Happy smiles, they fill the face
As play and laugh propel the day
And friendships grow in harmony
To see the joy in every way.

Candles burn when lights go out
But special light transforms the night
As Earth masks Moon from Sunny rays
Providing an ecliptic sight.

Thoughts swim by in lows and highs
Changing with the turning tide
As open hearts begin to sing
And Indian sunshine filters in.

A Seat With Ganesha

A seat with Ganesha
For stories of old
Surrounded by ruins -
Rustic, and gold.

A place of magnificence
It serves to astound
With beauty unparalleled -
In awe, I am bound.

To this scene of destruction
Where relics remain
My eyes fill with wonder
My heart senses pain.

For the loss of a city
Remarkably born
Now distant in past -
Its life, I am drawn.

To its shadow and light
Its spirit and soul
This crumbled scene
Where the sacred unfolds.

Fragile is the butterfly

An intimate beauty
Of symmetrical eyes
Patterns fragile wings.

Etched in silver
Framed with black
Her essence is displayed.

As gentle flutter
Wisps the sky
In feminine parade.

She'll touch your heart
And hold your smile
When you see her free.

With sacred bliss
In harmony
For all the world to see.

But beauty only lasts so long
It crumbles into night
As colours fade, and eyes close down
She leaves without a fight.

Lakshmi's Life

A life so gentle -
Calm and peace
Her living life
Is spent with ease.

Her ears of old
Enjoy the breeze
Her eyes so soft
They humble me.

Her gentle heart
Loves simple things:
A river wash
Is all she needs.

It soothes her soul
With ebb and flow
Her trunk moves free -
She truly knows.

That just some time
Spent in the sun
Is far too nice
To not have fun.

Thoughts in Bloom

I wander through my fields of thought
Searching for a bulb to plant -
A seedling of a good idea
To grow a creeping bloom.

Little gnomes of doubt bounce free
Tempting me from garden's gate
To plant a life on solid ground
And bury dreams away.

A weeded patch; potential born
But soon, the weeds are back again -
Strangling thoughts of freedom's flight
That birds above display.

A little spray to kill the weeds
Has willows weeping down on me
For they have grown to show the way -
The light for me to live each day.

For bouncing gnomes and wicked weeds
Will always make remark
But in a garden, as free as mine
The plants shall grow with spark.

<u>Love</u>

Illusion's Devotion

Within my dreams
You visit me -
Words of desire
Emerging through haze.

Two souls are connect
In loving exchange
But morning arrives
And the details fade.

Mellow mood
In sunshine's pink
Brings thoughts of you
To vision's view.

A messenger's gift -
Your heart to mine
Wrapped in space
As time subsides.

But stir me cold
With warm intent
For what is here
Is time well spent.

As dreams are made
Of beauty's lair
But lived alone
One's life is bare.

Scent of a stranger

In intimate space
I sensed his face
A loving presence
Of desirable essence.

A stranger's face -
His scent unknown
But follow close
And I'd be shown.

Through a window of light
By a mysterious force
To a searching gaze
Of a lover's plight.

His face transpired
To know me well
From a time ago
Or a magical spell.

He caught my thoughts
And held them tight
To search my soul
And find my light.

His loving arms
Caressed the scene
Freeing glory
Of mythical theme.

Where truth is found
In warm embrace
And open heart
Brings Godly grace -

I sense his rhythm;
Its growing pace
I love his heart
And I kiss his face.

Lover's Blossom

Desire's cup consumes a soul
Pouring lust through longing veins
Igniting with a spark of flame
Burning effervescently.

Supple, cherry-blossomed lips
Part to share a keeper's bloom
Seeking cherished sentiment
In adoration's arms.

Doors of sight, they softly close
Sealing a sacred sense of bliss
As gentle breeze is sensual breath
Preparing for a lover's kiss.

For taste feels a longing touch
Of succulent sensual chemistry
The poise of hurried, bated breath
Releases gushing mystery.

A melting sense creates a trance
Removing thought from lover's arms
As all of time escapes the scene -
Coating love in symphony.

Amber's warmth

Amber eyes of golden hue
Flicker lashes lit with lust
Creating an enchanting glow
That only joining-lovers know.

Heat that warms her precious skin
Puts winter's distance in the past
As envelopes; his arms become:
Sealing in her gifts.

Devouring each of every word
Their hunger grows into a thirst
With every longing, gentle gasp
That binds them in each other's grasp.

A soothing brush of skin-on-skin
Tingles hairs erect in play
Engaging their enamoured beat
For scenes of love's display.

Cherished Love

It took a while
To get to know
All you are
Beyond the show.

A beauty born
In to your skin
You share with me
Your heart within.

You touched my heart
You stroked my mind
You set me loose
To keep me kind.

And with this gift
We're now entwined
To share our love -
The strongest bind.

Our love is strong
Our love is deep
Let's cherish this -
Our love's for keeps.

Converging Paths

Our paths met:
Converging lines -
We came together
With fire inside.

Our bodies bound -
Two souls collide
In love of sorts
No shame to hide.

We shared so much
In play and speech
You touched my heart
With all you teach.

For you were there
With all your might
To share your love
And show me light.

But from the start
I saw your spirit
So I loved your heart
But I let you live it.

Distant Love

I loved him the distance
Over land and sea
And blankets of stars
Of different halves.

A tape couldn't measure
The depth of my pleasure
To see him again
For all we could be.

In matching halves
To link our past
Of losing sense
In love's intent.

Through looks of lust
That long for more
Indiscreet on a street
In close embrace.

But different times
In different halves
Make distant hearts
Run tragically.

And life's too short
To dwell in hope
Of matches sparked
So distantly.

Meandering Souls

You appeared one day -
In to my life:
A tower of strength
In physical form.

But clash caused crash
Through latent anger:
Fight and flight
Arrived like thunder.

But when the storm
Had found its calm
I placed my heart
Inside your palm.

And with your love
You held it soft;
You spoke the words
I longed to hear.

You cherished me
You grew my strength;
Showed me beauty
Of who I am.

But you are yours
And I am mine;
Together briefly
For reason's time.

Wandering hearts
We meet and part;
Meandering -
We'll always be.

And fond I am
Of all you are
We're meant to last
But drift and pass.

And thus it seems
I know your heart
But keep it free
To burn its spark.

Light In Your Sadness

The dark of sadness in your eye
Reflects a pain you hold inside
Resisting my unbridled urge
To mend your heart that breaks me.

The sorrow in your dampened heart
Reveals the pain you seem to bleed
In words across your troubled face
Unaware you need me.

The pain of torture wrecks your bones
Crumbled is your posture;
From years of hiding in your skin -
Closing off your heart.

My love to you is always here
Providing you with light relief;
From all your peril, and alarm -
Safety, in my arms.

And love you; only as you are -
As deep as you can trust
But open full I am to you
Despite your hurt distrust.

For slowly, love will open you
To all of life's delights
And hand-in-hand I'll hold you
In spirit and in strife.

A Garden's Love Story

Gilded gates of regal arms
Frame a meadow fit for kings
Guarded strong by fleeting stags
Light in living melody.

Palatial gardens terrace tales
Of memories gone by -
Sprung to life in Alice Bloom
To please the passing eye.

For petal buds reveal a story
Romancing in the spring
Of royal-rich encounters
That fertilise the beds -

Of gardens holding memories
Locked in loving history;
The wind provides a whisper
Of stories cased in gold.

For people that have gone now -
Only books providing lies
Of love that is amiss now -
Only flowers left in kind.

Pain

Birthed sadness

A soul is born
In to a Womb
Of fluid, warm divine.

But once it's birthed
The Elements
Can bruise its fragile skin.

Abusive Torrents
Swell that Soul
To form a tragic tale.

Of Blanket Sadness
Darkened Days -
No goodness to prevail.

And life flows on
In futile turns
Demeaning, all the while.

As lights turn out
And warmth turns cold
The heart, it runs a mile.

Innocent bouquet

He smelled my innocent bouquet
And found his way to taste me
With subtle charm I could not see
He worked his way to sway me.

In friendship's trust there was a lie -
He bargained with my heart
To have his way with little say;
My virgin soul forsaken.

I melted from my sense of youth
Lost in depths of my demise;
He'd groomed my fate from my control:
My life's protection failed me.

But years passed by in strength of self
As shame ran through its subtle course;
Rising from a hidden sphere
I sensed its light escape.

Experience is all its worth -
I smile it gently on its way
And sense its validated point;
Its pain will never shape me.

Dance of deceit

A delicious companion
Glances your way -
Catching you senseless;
Absorbing your rays.

Your beauty astounds him;
You've captured his mind
He's guiding your journey
He's leading you blind –

To a meal of illusion
A scene of display
Where mirrors are smoky
And life is displaced.

He watches you fade;
Your senses decline -
Through spellbound possession
And subtle demise.

He wants your resources:
You're trapped in his mind
Deceiving your angel;
His devil unwinds.

Too late to retract now
You're locked in his vice:
Your future is set now -
It doesn't look nice.

Triumphant Sleuth

In his love
That slept away
Emptiness prevailed.

In stories told
To strike my sense;
To think he didn't stray.

I barked a tree -
The wrong he said
But tree there seemed to be.

A foolish game
He thought he'd won
But overlooked my sleuth.

For cocky were his eyes I saw -
They beamed a liar's truth.

So bark once more
And truth was found
Beneath another tree.

When all revealed
He lost his shield
And cowardice transpired.

I said goodbye
And fled so free
To all that I desired.

A bullied tale

I did not see
In front of me
A spellbound tide
Of mystery.

I did not see
In front of me
A plan at work
To capture me.

A plan en route
For my demise -
Young, naïve
I wasn't wise.

A boy himself -
But different beast
He knew his way
With competence.

He pushed his way
In to my life
He didn't care -
I had no choice.

Fear ripped through
My fragile skin
I went along
But I was gone.

He took my heart
He ripped it out
He stamped on it
And laughed out loud.

Caged Heart

Life goes on
In every way -
I wake to face
The changing day.

Around my heart
There is a cage -
Bound so tight
I feel it ache.

I know it's true
That things will change
I just need time
To lose the pain.

Ivy's Tangle

A creeping ivy
Pains your heart -
It squeezes tight
With hurtful might.

You feel its grip
Repress your fire
No breath of life -
You lose desire.

Its gentle creep
Takes subtle form
Blinding you
From first it's born.

And as it grows
It seeps in deep
It wounds your heart
And cuts its beat.

With all the pain
It causes you
You cry restrained
But not in vain.

For when your fire
Knows all its worth
It burns the ivy
Off the earth.

As strength of heart
Cuts ivy's tangle
Freeing self
From torture's mangle.

Author Bio

In 2010, Marie launched www.picouture.com whilst photographing Winter Olympic cultural events in Vancouver. This site is her photographic portfolio, her blog, and the platform that she used to launch her poems.

At the end of 2011, Marie left England to travel to India. Whilst there, she was able to dive deeper into her loves of photography, writing, and yoga. She trained to be a yoga teacher whilst there, documented her journey in image and word, and began her deepest exploration of poetry.

Now that Marie is back in England the beautiful journey continues.

To find out more about Marie, head to her two websites:

www.picouture.com
www.marieskilling.com

www.ingramcontent.com/pod-product-compliance
Lightning Source LLC
Chambersburg PA
CBHW060058050426
42448CB00011B/2518